RAGDOLL CAT

Everything You Need To Owning, Housing, Feeding, Breeding, And Taking Proper Care Of Ragdoll Cat

ALEX DWAYNE

Table of Contents

CHAPTER ONE 3

INTRODUCTION...3

CHAPTER TWO 5

BRIEF HISTORY OF RAGDOLLS CAT.................5

CHAPTER THREE....................................7

TAKING PROPER CARE OF RAGDOLL CAT.......7

CHAPTER FOUR 16

RAGDOLL BEHAVIOR AND TEMPERAMENT .16

CHAPTER FIVE 19

MORE FACT ABOUT RAGDALL CAT 19

CHAPTER SIX 23

ADOPTING A CAT FROM RAGDOLL CAT.......23

THE END...25

CHAPTER ONE

INTRODUCTION

The Ragdoll cat is a large type of cat, maximum widely known due to its easygoing and mellow nature. They've prolonged, thick fur jackets and markings that appear like a Siamese. Solving your ragdoll cat ought to involve a normal feeding and grooming time table, collectively with regular appointments with the vet for checkups and vaccinations. For right care of your ragdoll cat, they'll be healthy, happy, together

with a higher lively puppy which
you ought to revel in.

CHAPTER TWO

BRIEF HISTORY OF RAGDOLLS CAT

The Ragdoll breed isn't pretty 50 years vintage. The cats were created in California in 1963. Breeder Ann Baker desired to develop a stunning cat with a loving, mild personality, and she began with home longhairs of unknown ancestry. Josephine, the foundation cat, changed into white with Siamese-kind markings, and in her genes she carried a seal mitted or black tuxedo pattern. The Ragdolls of today descend from Josephine and her son, Daddy Warbucks, in addition to other unknown domestic longhair adult males.

The Cat Fanciers association started registering Ragdolls in 1993, and that they achieved championship repute in 2000. Today Ragdolls are the 5th maximum popular breed registered via CFA.

CHAPTER THREE

TAKING PROPER CARE OF RAGDOLL CAT

Feeding

Clean water and food are absolute requirements for the Ragdoll. It's cautioned that a person constantly has a bowl filled with dry food easily to be had for your cat, similarly to a bowl of unpolluted water. Wet meals are maximum probable not essential every day; however it's genuinely your choice, and simply what your ragdoll prefers. You can need to test out one-of-a-kind manufacturers and flavors of wet meals. It can provide greater vitamins and add variety on your ragdoll's weight loss plan. We suggest feeding your ragdoll most of the top class brands of meals because the exceptional is higher. Commonly, kittens need to have a unique formulation of meals, test collectively with your vet or nearby puppy shop in case you're not positive.

Progressively alter smooth water bowl every day, and also the meals bowl whenever viable to avoid bacteria and germs from amassing.

Grooming

Ragdoll jackets can vary thick and haired. The normal ragdoll locks are incredibly thick and rather tender to touch. The dimensions of the fur could be medium to prolong.

They often perform an excellent task of grooming themselves out on every other require immoderate brushing. It may be useful to easy them strenuously a few occasions in keeping with week to keep away from matting from the fur. Every other purpose at the back of brushing on the everyday schedule is in case you search for a knot growing, it is simple to sweep it earlier than it receives unmanageable.

Ragdolls generally tend to enjoy grooming and will let you actually brush away!

Bathing

Bathing isn't required if ordinary grooming is done. It is probably tremendous to offer your ragdoll a bath a few activities yearly, to scrub the coat if simply dirty or must they have got end up something which cannot be brushed out.

Make certain that you hire a shampoo and conditioner that's formulated mainly for cats, as regular human merchandise is probably risky for your ragdoll.

Claws

Declawing the cat is a questionable problem and something which brings a variety of opinions. We don't suggest declawing a ragdoll unless of direction, it will assist using the safety interior a household, in particular with kids. Clipping the claws can be finished frequently to prevent damage on your furnishings or some other products within the home, so if that's your predominant motive in the back of declawing the kitty, your preference ought to be considered cautiously since it isn't reversible.

Bear in mind while a ragdoll cat is declawed, it should be constrained in its contact with the outside global. Without front claws, a ragdoll does not have a variety of protection against other creatures or threats it'd come upon.

Cat clutter container

The cat clutter box ought to be stored in a enormously secluded region to match privacy, even though now not so looked after that it's far hard to get entry to easy. Commonly, a laundry room or some other spare room can serve as exquisite vicinity.

We endorse scooping out within this area at the least one time every day and replacing the litter weekly. For those who have several cats, then it is probably vital to easy this area times every day, morning and night for example.

There are various manufacturers and kinds of clutter available it's some preference. The number one element is to discover something which your cat uses, is straightforward to help hold neat and lower priced for the budget.

Vet

You need to bring your ragdoll to some vet often based on the matters they suggest. You may need to get vaccination shots after which any whatever else in an effort to hold the cat safe and healthy.

There might be special elements in case your ragdoll spends time beyond regulation outdoors, for instance, pest management alongside a greater inclination in the direction of sickness. Make certain you speak this together

along with your vet and exercising
a time table which makes feel.

CHAPTER FOUR

RAGDOLL BEHAVIOR AND TEMPERAMENT

Ragdolls are from time to time nicknamed "puppy cats" because of the way they observe their people from room to room. Now not even the bathroom offers privacy from this sort of mild love bugs. In contrast to many cats, their favored position isn't always on excessive however one that gives human contact: at the ground mendacity for your toes, at your face on the sofa or, ideally, for your lap. Now not for this cat the curtain-hiking shenanigans or boisterous video games of chase of other breeds. Ragdolls have a slight electricity stage and a laidback demeanor. These are the cats you'll see being dressed up in infant garments and pushed round in a baby buggy by way of the youngsters. They're now not loud, speaking in a voice described as tender and musical.

The Ragdoll continues his kitten like playfulness into adulthood and vintage age. He enjoys an excellent sport of fetch and can be inclined to learn to stroll on a leash. He should stay thoroughly indoors in which he's covered from sickness and vehicles.

CHAPTER FIVE

MORE FACT ABOUT RAGDALL CAT

All cats have the capability to develop genetic health problems, just as all of us have the capability to inherit a specific disorder. Any breeder who claims that her breed or lines has no fitness or genetic problems is either mendacity or isn't informed approximately the breed. Run, don't walk, from any breeder who does not offer a fitness guarantee on kittens, who tells you that the breed is 100 percent wholesome and has no recognized issues, or who tells you that her kittens are isolated from the principle a part of the household for health motives.

Ragdolls are typically wholesome, but bladder stones and a coronary heart circumstance referred to as hypertrophic cardiomyopathy are among the situations which have been stated within the breed.

Hypertrophic cardiomyopathy (HCM) is the maximum commonplace form of heart sickness in cats. It causes thickening (hypertrophy) of the coronary heart muscle. An echocardiogram can verify whether a cat has HCM. Researchers have identified the genetic mutation that causes the development of HCM inside the Ragdoll and feature developed a genetic test that permits breeders to screen cats before breeding them. Cats identified with HCM must be eliminated from breeding packages. Keep away from breeders who claim to have HCM-unfastened strains. No one can assure that their cats will in no way develop HCM.

Ragdoll kittens will have fast growth spurts and it's essential for them to have plenty of meals to be had all the time. in case your

Ragdoll kitten cleans his plate, offer him a touch greater until he stops eating. Once the cat reaches his full size at 4 years, then you may ration his meals so he doesn't get fat.

CHAPTER SIX

ADOPTING A CAT FROM RAGDOLL CAT

A breeder isn't your handiest choice for obtaining a Ragdoll. Even though Ragdoll kittens are almost in no way located in shelters and rescue, person Ragdolls, both pedigreed and combined, aren't continually so lucky. You can find the right Ragdoll in your circle of relatives thru Ragdoll Cat Breed Rescues or via checking your local shelters. Anyplace you got your Ragdoll, ensure you have a terrific contract with the seller, shelter or rescue organization that spells out responsibilities on each sides. In states with pet "lemon legal guidelines," be sure you and the character you get the cat from both apprehend your rights and recourses.

Kitten or grownup, take your Ragdoll for your veterinarian soon after adoption. Your veterinarian could be able to spot troubles, and could paintings with you to set up a preventive routine to help you avoid many fitness issues.

THE END